The Popular Vote

Poems by Star Black

saturnalia books

Distributed by Independent Publishers Group
Chicago

for Bill Knot

Saturnalia Books
105 Woodside Rd.
Ardmore, PA 19003
info@saturnaliabooks.com

ISBN: 978-1-947817-04-3
Library of Congress Control Number: 2018910480

Book Design by Robin Vuchnich
Printing by Versa Press
Cover Art: Robin Vuchnich

Distributed by:
Independent Publishers Group
814 N. Franklin St.
Chicago, IL 60610
800-888-4741

Acknowledgements

I am grateful to the Parrish Art Museum for inviting me to write new poems for the People's State of the Union event, held in February 2017 and 2018, by attending story circles of citizens sharing their views on current events, which resulted in "Election Shock" and "Juice News." I wish to thank Albert Mobilio for asking me to write poems on a chosen topic for the *Double Take Reading Series* at apexart with the poet Joseph Donahue who selected a small exhibition of 19th century paintings at The Morgan Library entitled "Sky Studies." Thanks also to Yaddo for the time to write "An Elegy" and to Christopher Salerno, Henry Israeli and Robin Vuchnich. Two titles in the book, "Noncommittal Shrubbery" and "Citadel of Dampness" are phrases in poems by John Ashbery found in Library of America's *Ashbery: Collected Poems 1991-2000*.

Table of Contents

I. ELECTION SHOCK

II. A SLOW WHIRL

III. JUICE NEWS

IV. SKY STUDIES

V. AN ELEGY

THE POPULAR VOTE

I

ELECTION SHOCK

HISTORY TOO SOON

The living room
is in a burrowed mood, like a Diane
Arbus photo of a Christmas tree

with detonating gifts. Rhyme riffs
as jazz blares from the Batmobile, its edgy
tires swiveling the avenues. To carry a sign,
to be real, to wait and see, to multiply

the options of acute anxiety,
is as quotidian as the moon outside the living
room that has now become a monochromatic square,
the election served on TV trays

like a granite biscuit. Who can eat?
Who can promise the ocean a deck chair,
a Frisbee? The margins of suffering squeeze.
Halos drop to the asphalt and ping.

ELECTION SHOCK

I know you have
your laundry list of paranormal errands.
I know you have your paddleboat and your paradox,
which is petunia-shaped and ambiguous
and twitchy,

but are you fastened
to the screen of near-eternity?
Its meatloaf recipes with a tiny American flag
stuck in raw beef?

If not, you are tampering
with the evening by going to sleep early
or by making love or by being lonely,
and you have yet to see

the stranger with a red tie,
the consequences of chopped onion,
bread crumbs and a cow,

you have yet to envelop
forgotten arias and the dystopia of hope.
You need to bake. You need to serve

meatloaf.

SHOCK TWO

One likes a semi-circle of commentators
to deploy evaluations in quick, consternated
discussions on stocks and deportations.
One likes bleak, ragged perimeters,
fuzzy in dreams, but important,

like an opposite current
in a grey river flowing into one's eyes,
making the view
irreducible, artless and innocent,
for a New York minute.

How modern airport poisoning is.
One would think the noon-time sun
would be leveling like a nap,
that a splattered bathrobe by Jim Dine
would be just that, nothing more
than cloth and paint,

yet the screens permeate
the Hubble Telescope's wide-ranging
overview with queasy hubris
that magnifies more than carefree stars,
novas with other things to do.

Telephones are through.
Only heads of state use them

and they don't even talk that much,
too busy poisoning or golfing.

But, no, one must be patient,
one must wear plaid, a baleful interlacing
of color. Screens are no longer black and white.
They have an acrylic flavor,
an encaustic-tile feel.

Well, see you on the carsick road
to Mexico or Canada,
see you in the dot dot dot of monomania.
You won't come? You're sticking it out?
Peace be with you.

SHOCK THREE

The sundial is so convenient
it appears inebriated.
Days are a phone directory no one reads,
an off-season Slurpee too cold to drink,
but why listen to me?

You need the brightness of hair,
chopper-blade strategy. Let's see:
trombones ache on the makeshift sidelines.
Cities are measurable, yet faint.
Unsung pages missed the last auction,
they crinkle at your feet,
matted by dust-caked boots after 9/11.

A salesman passes an embassy. No one is around.
Diplomats park their cars anywhere, then leave.
You say you feel "unfelt-up and driven."
Go on. I'm listening.
The past just vanished.
They sold it at the auction.

RUBBLE

The pressure of being wrong
is overwhelming. Rhetoric used to be
like furniture. One could sit down.
One could read. One could gallop the beach
at twilight like Lady Godiva in a comic
strip, a nude superhero
stepping out on her husband.
Now the pipes are hissing,
the wattage is blown.
The evening is a kidnapped kid
locked in a cargo container
as vultures organize population density.
A magic wand could set things free,
we could start over,
but the sublime wouldn't like it, too facile,
too startled by fantasy rather than
criminal justice. Must this be
only a marsh of diminishing size,
lost egrets alighting in gated communities?
Perhaps one is missing something
violet in the pastels. Perhaps
the rainbow is too pale.
Are you in physical therapy now?
I miss you madly.

LEDGERS

Handwriting has always been
lemon-colored when categorized–
so many categories, so few quills, yet
the sky is kind. It is beyond sprawling.
It's nonprofessional. Do you mind
if I breathe into a sieve? Gullies
puzzle me. Motorcades blur
my clear view of the big Inaugural Parade,
so many motorcycles gliding by in slow motion,
Secret Service men who look like Breaking Bad
crack dealers with day jobs, staring
back at me as I wait in the bleachers
for palomino equestrians
to tip their cowboy hats to the Prez
who will then complain for two weeks
there were not enough me's watching him.
I don't believe everything revealing
is perverted. I think we need manicures.
I like re-phrasing at random shelters.
It can add up, even if no one
sees your hands.

BLUE PAVEMENT

One opts out of dark glasses,
becomes less glistery, less suave.
I would say unaffected, but I can't.
The orchard is too splendid, the apples
too red, and memory makes tomorrow
none the wiser unless the blinkers slip. You,
for example, are a natural-born
library trustee. You can
un-chain-link me. You can contradict
stressed-out runners-up, check out their book,
return it on time, no fee, no clutter.
Remorse will leave you like a sad sack shape-shifting
into a jadeite rose. You may find
a late date, a dancer. People will again say
something you can hear. An odyssey will appear.
Yours. You take up weaving. You re-read
Philomela's sad tale outside the classroom.
You are fortunate. You are longed for.
The country is back in style.
The noise left.

FAUX SOLO

Can another person be an
arrondissement? Can one live
in an apartment with French doors
on the penultimate floor
behind a facade of sandstone
and have a conversation about
overriding the system?
Conditions intrude like a pixilation of rain
or an intervention. One catches a bus,
attends a lecture on antique illustrations
showing third-world savages in loincloths,
as if missionaries thought they needed help.
One becomes grooved by input, by flak-speak.
The globe isn't so sure. It has doubts.
One turns around, yearns for a theory
to hide in, of anagrammatic difficulty
like an astounding football diagram,
or a half-erased Sol DeWitt wall,
or the multiple arcs of an eagle's claw,
something traipsey–and then goes home,
empty. A gullible staircase awaits,
uncarpeted. Wood is fine, Bounty-dusted
with Murphy's soap, but all staircases
look alike. What then? Perhaps,
you can make a suggestion, initiate
a fuzzed aura with no answer.

SLANTWARD

En route to a shore of tasseled harps,
the ocean lifelike and holy, bathers clock
in and go through customs. The dunes vibrate.
Aardvarks hide under shells. Maidens on ponies
dwell in the dark. They have a lot of company—
sheriffs, headlines, advice. They call these
ambient nights feather-wise. Lucent
ghosts are unrelenting. There

are no demurring trees, just pebble
claimants and unfettered fish. They stay
away. The future collapses, stops tapping its
cane. Whitecaps peddle their sewing machines
of air. Life expectancy is outpaced by the moment,
its chorus of trance dependency and salt. Five-o'clock
shadows are unbalkanized and friendly. Errands
don't nettle, bicycles sink. What's at hand

is bland, uncorseted like zillions
of liters of liquid, supple. Far removed from
litigation, the beach sits around, unclassifiable,
neither self-deprecating nor swift.

MOOD MOUNTAINS

An old shade in the form of rats
spelled backwards carted me off in
a patterned shawl to Schenectady
where humor ended during

the depression. The return is
altering. Nothing can be cozy or
reinvented. You can't assault a blow-dry
or jump ship. You're stuck. Skeletal
fingers tingle your back

like the tip of a flyswatter.
You're back, yet not back. You're
malingering. Once you were derivative
now you can't sing. Neighborhoods
have a tornado-blown feeling,

as if you thought you needed
to know what "polysyndeton" meant.
Meanwhile, "naught" is skyrocketing
into a collusion of naughts.

Naught should be only a word,
not close friends, a gang rape, a taking,
yet who are you to say whether anyone
has gone away or what is clay or
what is senseless wondering?

NONCOMMITTAL SHRUBBERY

The reason yards don't work, mine,
is because I never find the time to seed
and re-seed and sprinkle. I wanted to grow
what I didn't need to mow. I wanted

groundcover: vinca, pachysandra,
periwinkle, dichondra, moss. I wanted
part-time rains, dimensional greens, nothing
blade-like and stained by canine pee,

nothing connoting a toll bell on a hill,
just a would-be verdant over-spill in tumbled
disarray, but I asked too much from thunder.
My peripheries are elusive. My greens

are motley, of motley ilk. Your grass
is green and smooth like silk, consistently
improved. I never see it behind your hedges
but perhaps I'll visit your driveway soon.

WISTFUL

The unavoidable sunset is a featurette
of the postmarked vistas where nothing
improves the past, when sex was best with
unacknowledgement and boombox regrets
didn't last, when there were no holdovers,
no brisk quarrels, just nap times and

succotash, before anyone had tasted
an artichoke or sipped clouds through
a straw. Ancient times were last Tuesday,
a trompe-l'oeil of mist. Carpenters were
dog-tired and never shaved. Fleas lit
up as fireflies without ticks. Streets

were graceful. Now the spaceship's
cut in half, yet you still shimmer, eyeing
pharmacies with a smile. You left your
scepter in the aisle. A buzz of retrieval
follows. The fountains wink.

CITADEL OF DAMPNESS

The old grey lady used to come out
once a day. Now she's an intermittent affliction.
One feels like Goldie Locks chopping down trees,
tending a dying need to hold newsprint in sections.
Painful moments, mindful of azaleas underfoot,
collect postage stamps as native art,

obsolescently, while missing the last train
to informed sanity. One resists, becomes a minimalist,
pours triangles of sand onto a polished floor, seeks
a lake shore, a currency diversion, a warrant to
relax. But where's the poignancy and can it
outlast progress? Take a wild guess.

II

A SLOW WHIRL

COUNTERVALENCE

Bitterness, like innocence, dwindles.
Everyone moves into a city of chasubles
and nerves, to say "hi" to traffic, swingeingly,
but there's more to do than to misunderstand
inventory. Snow falls through the window.
The paint thinner looks happy, waiting.

As a dolphin in a cab, one courts rejection
but a kiss of calmness weighs down jots on
a napkin with a new plan, something pivotal
before the dusk of television, a solitary
dialogue with a music stand, stones

resting on its top rather than a sheet
from a sonata. A Tobago watercolor could
be resting there, too, staring into space above
the bartender, looking like a humble must-do
accomplishment. I think of you, our days when
plastic bottles didn't rim the Mediterranean
and refuse in Rome's river was less

durable, a disappearing swishiness.
Worries, semi-persuasive, were less journaled,
the open road less mini-Malled by stoplights. You
never liked tongs, throngs, or one upmanship.
You knew it would all come to this, a heron
indoors forsaking swankiness.

UNSUBSCRIBER

A small-town swimmer listens
for the benumbed wrecking ball to
demolish all heights but cornerstones,
the weather a landfill of bygones,
the creek a soupy blue, wavelets
mewling, longitudes

undeserving of you, pleasant
moonshine. A stumbling breeze
braces itself against a bumble bee,
moving through the loss of you,
your disbelieving clamor,
your assured bedrock

devouring candle wax in
low flames below groundbreaking
clouds. How loud your absence is
in this muddled know-how that
is too uncrowded without you
like a creek without water.

A SHELL, ONCE

You out-smoothed diversion,
ousted all emulsions, no one could
see the rollicking engineer tinkering
with indivisibles, the otherwise of now
in the assuagement of exile. The moon,
tidying up expectantly, swan dives
through double-flips to miss
the earth, to appear mild.

Such incidents lie, like a cracked
shell, within wet sand. She had hideaways,
took out garbage, waited in the sea for
sustenance, her fidelities fed by tides,
but she's crunched in a pantomime
of seasides, in life.

MAETERLINCK

A dream of plurals that cannot be penetrated
by the ousted world is lost to sunlight. Cement
and veils return, the ripple-effect of hunger.

What seemed astonishing is just another
Aurora, a day of soba noodles and incrementals.
The immortalizing caress that accommodated

you is washed out like the Pleiades by light.
You are many selves again: the parking lot,
the cheap flight, the smoothed-out mattress,

a bat in a hat in Madrid, if Madrid matters,
as well. It is just best not to tell anyone you're
traveling. They like committees and groceries.

CHECK POINT

Can there be leftovers from a reverie,
strands of misconstrued accuracy, something
less familiar than childhood details–a lost shoelace,
a squeamish homecoming to an old trike,
pop-up mammoths, something

useful without a miracle like timid lightning?
Militancy is nuts, swarming through bomb-demolished
walls, shellshock-shepherds cramming queued gates
toward peace. It's late-ish and only beginning.
We never seem to wash the streets.

ODE TO JOHN

Midsummer shambles, their winsome anxieties,
disclosures that fit through a keyhole precisely,

make afternoons the renovations of a nervous room
that wafts upon flotsam and seals on salted loam

in an unmoored houseboat afloat on calibrated seas,
gulls suspended in implied dives far from any city

where grief escapes saw-toothed reefs and slides into
unalarming recesses in a hushed release from stress,

from insecurity, then ambles above danger safely. No
one is at fault as the days grow slower and the hull

breaks apart, splintering the water with new prayers,
the gulls unacclaimed, unaware, without shadows

to hide under. Carefulness, resistance to numbness, is
the elemental tide that lifts ships into the air and deposits

them ashore. You've always liked walking the beach,
lolling portside with the stevedores. Now it is time

for averages to slink in, leveling the rhythmic fun
as the one-hundred-percent odds of life takes its tally.

Still, without you, there is only memory, not enough
action. You've always seen through me, waving

behind a scrim of illogical precision; you've never
been remiss or rude. At least, I've tried to understand you

in this see-you-soon lullaby of civil discourse, aporia's
limpid force, and I am, of course, dreaming this up.

SEMI-TERRAINS

I live beneath a farthingale
like a Magritte torso surrounded
by hoops. My height is modest, my mind
unassuming, concave. I'm often missed
by those who dance away, baffled by
poppy seeds beaded on gossamer.

Mostly I've an irrevocable need
to sashay on the surface of the sea
under the rain. Are you still getting old
again? Are your lambent companions
bricklaying the winter season?
The ballroom passes away,

no, faints or swoons. It feels willowy
in the diorama as if it withheld too many
complaints to remain horizontal and became
waves of parquet, dreamlike, uneasy. Floors
get that way under dancers and dance
away, too. Not me, I still see you.

QUARRY QUERY

Is there a whole story to the future of Friday
or could it be the last time flesh envelops me,
a verge into unknown consistency, a radiance,

or, in case there isn't, since "is" or "isn't" doesn't
exist within the soul's eminence, its piece-of-the-pie
slice of dimensionlessness, its outta-here oomph,

can a whole story be entirely elsewhere other
than now, without cloud barriers? One always asks,
reconsiders permanence later in life, reconsiders

romance when least able to consider it, thus
the "re" as in remembering, the "re" in redux, yet
second thoughts could be a shadow of radiance,

an emissary of Friday earlier in the week,
an improbable à bientôt, like handwriting on
water just for today, not for the end of time.

THE VIEW

Targets retire
behind concertina wire
uncontained by rapture like billboards
on a visual scroll of blasted abodes.

Our dividends almost barge in,
our gnatty drones, as we adjust dust
with a bullwhip. Aleppo's own are stopped
at the airport and thrown back home,

a prison of displacement.
Disgrace closes each page of our daybook.
Tomorrow is a second look, a stun gun
in an echo.

III

JUICE NEWS

THE POPULAR VOTE

Glass-ceiling balloons,
why did you never fall? Why
were the wide, expansive rafters
at the Javits Center just too tall?

How did locker-room sleaze
prevail over Tammy Wynette? Why
is the middle word in the convention slogan
 "Love Trumps Hate" the only one
we can never forget?

How did soundness of mind
deposit us on the footfalls
of a long red tie? Why were Rubio's
fingers short and why does a golf
course in Scotland still matter?

Did we vote for labeled water,
privatizing thirst? Do our rivers hurt,
as our eyes tire of watching
progress in reverse?
Could we have a stable genius
driving a long, dark hearse to a gravesite
with all of us in it?

Glass-ceiling balloons,
balloons of poise and experience,
was your "basket of deplorables" too stringent?
Did Comey's fast-ball slam you in the hip?
Did you listen to too many pollsters?
Did you dare to over-predict?

You were loyal to your staff
even one of their husbands dropped
his pants on the information highway
before a Prozac-addled nation.
You stayed calm, collected,
under-persuasive.

You didn't hire enough generals
nor did you weep.
Women don't share tears in public.
Now we don't sleep.

MELANIA'S ATTIRE AS SHE ENTERS THE ROTUNDA TO HEAR THE STATE OF THE UNION ADDRESS, JANUARY 30, 2018

The white pantsuit doesn't dance,
it is reserved after bearing a child.
Buxom mistresses are horny and wild,
the white pantsuit, pausing above the crowd,
is dignified, discreet, trance-like, complete.
It is pre-nupped and unwrinkled.
It conjures a reverie and must be stark,
not eggshell white or ivory or champagne,
which is pale, pale beige, but flaxen
and bright, brimming with
adamant control.

Democratic senators,
quiet as stone, slump in their chairs, and wear
DACA-protest black. The white pantsuit
floats intact, adrift in elegance, posing.
It doesn't wrinkle. It doesn't attack.
It is white as a dreamer
filtered through a blinkered country.
It overrides, with slender hips,
the debate wardrobe of a vanquished Hillary.
It will not be worn twice in public.
It is a symbol, a statement, most likely
okayed by Stephen Miller who most likely
wrote the upcoming speech on Hispanic gangs
in the ethical gutter, raping not only women
but our streets. The pantsuit gleams,
an overlay of bewitching power,
the power of compliant observation,
the power of a faint smile,
the power of stature.

STORMY SWATTING THE PRESIDENT ON 60 MINUTES, MARCH 25, 2018

At twenty-seven,
I knew how to play ball.
I watched golfers and accepted dinner invitations.
I am not tall but nor am I short
and I like horses.
I finance my own bankroll.
I listen to lawyers.
I understand my body
is an illusion that works
so I put it to work.
I am an equestrian.
I prove a high school yearbook
knows what it talks about.
I lose nothing.
I negotiate.
I have facts at my fingertips
and keep my hands on my lap
when interviewed.
At hotels, my hands are more relaxed.
I can be a Playboy Bunny
or give black-leather swacks.
I see the entire driven comedy of lust.
I have no problem with it.
It doesn't unnerve me.
It doesn't assault.
It doesn't even interest me.
I like horses.

And lawyers love me.
They want a percent of my experience,
something to take home.
I live in the fantasy economy
and it pays well.
I could be a waitress, a stable hand.
I could be a rollerballer, a bat out of hell,
but I like impermanence and distance.
I have a past my daughter will not know.
I am a movie director.
I meet budgets.
I believe in grass roots release,
the little man's horny times.
I am little.

TRUMP RETURNING FROM MAR-A-LAGO ALONE, MARCH 27, 2018

The frenzied blades of grass
below my helicopter as it lands
look ashen. I can't Tweet.
I'm a family man.
I have young and grown children.
The fake media has silenced my wife.
It's ruinous. Pure poison,
rancid as dead rats in a damp basement,
very bad.
I do charities, beauty contests.
I built a skating rink for everyday citizens.
I'm saving the country from itself
without Washington.
I'm removing drugs and scum.
I'm putting miners back to work,
lessening the tax burden of businessmen,
stopping the plunder from abroad,
the global pandemonium,
and can't even call a friend in Moscow
to congratulate him
without media muck, media bunk.
Even Sloppy Steve betrayed me
along with that horror of spectacles, Comey,
a cop without a country, total cad.
Pipelines, off-shore drilling, cheap gas–
I make them happen.
I'm not a criminal like Hillary.

I don't go after White House interns.
I'm not a hesitator like Obama.
I make plans,
round up illegal aliens,
send them back to the map.
My phone friends know I'm innocent,
doing my job, dining with donors,
protecting my son, solving
dead-end diplomacy problems
with an embassy move,
assigning guns to teachers.
I've got vision.
I'm social with the world
and everyone listens, except California.

TRUMP DENIES THE EXISTENCE OF DAVID DENNISON'S PAYMENT OF $130,000 TO PEGGY PETERSON, MARCH 29, 2018

Not my problem.
Don't know a thing.
Talk to my lawyer.
I call him at three in the morning.
We watch TV together.
He's on it. He's got a lawyer.
It's all slander. Give me a break.
I'm waiting for Kim Jung-un to return from China.
He's scared. He's on the run.
And the market?
What's one bashed-up car in a fatal accident?
Pennies. I'm reorganizing a swamp.
I've got Bolton. Big bombs.
I showed up at a PGA fundraiser in 2006
and what do I get?
A hoax.

MORE PRESIDENTIAL SILENCE ON STORMY

I've been told that I'm not involved,
that a nonexistent thug in a parking lot,
lifted out of a flabbergasting con-job script,
never happened. I'm calling Fox & Friends
to put it on hold. I can slow things down.
Michael, who handles a tiny bit
of my business, is a good man. He's taking
a three-month breather while I scrunch
the State Department and patch up
the howling match with North Korea
which, by the way, I won.

RAIDING THE OFFICES OF MICHAEL D. COHEN, APRIL 9, 2018

Officials at the F.B.I. don't retire early
nor do they easily comply with a rough-and-tumble bully.
Their agents invade his lawyer's stash if only to find an adulterer's alibi,
but that's enough for a day's work.
The agents' wives aren't worried.
No one is physically hurt.
It's just a drive uptown
in a city of tenants,
tenants who pay well, of course,
but the focus is on sex. Why not? It's easy.
It makes even D.A.s friendly.
Everything is paperwork when you obey the law,
dotting the i's, crossing the t's.
Everything is Twitterless and mute.
And Russians like sex, too,
according to a dossier no one can prove.

Agents return home from work,
tumble backwards onto a couch in the den.
It's been a long day for the F.B.I. but fatigue is welcome.
Administrations come and go,
like notches in bark on the backyard tree.
When you're trained to invade you need durability,
fitness and focus,
and home is a place to return to, crime-free.
It isn't Mar-a-Lago but it's comfy, and, tonight,
falling asleep will be easy.

CAMBRIDGE ANALYTICA IN FREEFALL

Multiplying therapists
recommend ninety days of abstinence
from digital delving to ameliorate not-a-wink,
leaving you with only secondary anxieties:
a thousand invisible cookies
implanted in your home computer.
And you thought you weren't
being watched while you were watching.
You thought you could just peep in at no charge,
keep apace with the endless ramifications
of an alleged golden shower
and your time was yours.
You weren't a dark-web statistic
in a global marketing empire.
You were free,
free as one-person-one-vote
democracy, free as "All men are created equal"
equality, with no "Me, too" revisions,
and not one cookie in the cloud could blind you.
You were all eyes, all ears.
You were elevating downtime.
Who knew you were a violated friend when you,
shy as ever, were just being social from afar?

Lucky you have a car
and can't friend and drive at the same time.
Maybe someone else is in it.
That would be nice.

SILICON APOLOGY: ZUCKERBERG TESTIFIES BEFORE CONGRESS, APRIL 10, 2018

I can't wait to shuck legal briefings
and return to what I know: sharing.
I'm facing a sea of suits on the East Coast
who can't distinguish gramophones from code,
making nice, and what do they ask–
who are my competitors?
They didn't understand me
a decade ago but I run the show.
I said so and I'm still saying it. With feeling.
Knowing them, they want yes-or-no privacy settings
and have just started streaming. I gotta go.
The buck stops here and I'll let you know
what I do. No worries. I was foolish.
I'm sorry. I'm putting a team of new hires on security.
Without manpower the Russians won't stop
and you're making immigration difficult,
but, never mind, it's your show, I'm contrite.

COMEY CLOBBERS TURPITUDE, BOOK LAUNCH, APRIL 12, 2018

Kissing the king's ring
was so creepy I lost my job.
Lordy, I believe in ethics.
Hillary's demise doesn't make me feckless.
It makes me thorough. It gives me
the right hug in the right world,
a world of probity and courage.
Her emails were questionable.
I questioned them. Enough said.
I moved on to a snake's red-hot bed
with its mob-infested code of loyalty.
I earned my excruciation and my dread
in the country's slide from purity,
its values a shredding-machine of insecurity.
Hillary? I made inquiries.
I closed them. I reopened them
late in the game.
I was "mildly nauseous", which
I have since corrected to "mildy nauscated"
upon learning these actions may have
damaged her campaign,
but I wasn't cowed and I wasn't blind.
I'd do it again.

INVADING SYRIA, WITH HELP, ON APRIL 13, 2018

In times of undue personal stress,
a war, if modest, is best. Headlines leap
into international exposure and the measured
voice of a seasoned general explaining precise targets hit,
within earshot of Damascus, gives a soothing lift
to mass fear and electoral trauma.
Slime balls be damned. Let them waddle
around on book tours. We aided and abetted
Saddam Hussein's Blessed Ramadan Offensive,
his issue with the Kurds, why not
punish Assad with our friends
the day after that dratted dossier
raised its pee-and-prostitutes head? It's timing.
We're throwing out the trash. And we're not alone.
The world is outraged by the use of mustard gas
banned after World War I, and we are, too.

Melania, I goofed, I strayed, I wandered.
Tonight I'm straight as an arrow.
Bolton's a boon. He organizes things
when I'm feeling most sorrowful.
I called Cohen. I'm taking care of it,
and the market's up two points this week.
You said to run or not to run.
I went for the job and I'm doing it.
Come close, Melania, relax.

THE POSSIBLE MUSINGS OF PUTIN AFTER THE U.S.-LED ALLIED STRIKE AGAINST SYRIA, APRIL 15, 2018

Nothing could be nicer
than another American disaster
like corralling the United Kingdom
and France into a Caucasian collaboration
against a Middle-Easterner.
If not a liberator, Assad is, at least, a leader,
filmed strolling into his office early the next morning–
slim, upright and polished–
allowing to the global press
that Russia's very own missiles
were deployed in his country's defense
and his counter-attack was a total success.

Duoma's a sidecar.
We don't want military victory,
we want duress. We aim to whittle away
western supremacy, step by step. First of all,
why use aerial power when there's
the internet? Why pull out
all the stops in Washington when Washington
is already in a mess, dancing around
my unflappable denials? Why release
sex details when there's already blackmail?
I liked the guy, his big deal of dealing.
We had business plans. He doesn't
have that caustic Cold War

feeling that plunders tax payers
with metastasizing investigative committees.
On the other hand, plundering
American citizens is interesting. Again,
I needn't do anything but stage a few family-like meetings
and then quell an ex-Secretary of State. One thing
that is free is withholding information
and those that have it should be left out of the equation.
At least, he was kind enough to acknowledge me
after my election. Pass me WikiLeaks.
Call the United Nations.

UNMECHANIZED DEATH TALLIES

In this land of disgruntled ex-employees,
a land of splintered advocacies, shivved candidates
and eleven Syrian refugees, night splices repose.
Some people fall asleep at dinner and wake up at one
in the morning to iron their clothes. Agitation,
ricocheting through groupspeak weeks
of television, disrupts dream patterns,
even if falling missiles are so very far away,
one hundred and three of them perfectly executed
in Syria during a "Mission Accomplished" replay
of a bomber-jacket-clad "Decider" on an aircraft carrier at sea.
April winds ripple through trees after a baffling winter.
Lonely forsythia sprigs emit a modicum of yellow,
the sky still wearing its gray cape.
Tomorrow's another day. Thirsty-Thursday's bars
in the city will be packed with Bernie's armies seeking hormonal
release from facts. All continues as we wait
for a perfectly-executed counterattack
and not from Xi. He's mollifying. He doesn't need
our soybeans that much. He runs a developing country
that's developing. The Third World stretch is shrinking,
but, lucky for us, Kellyanne Conway has returned,
burning with ire. There's not only one
"Light my Fire" songster within our flanks.
We have more than one flamingo in this dark party.
We're not folding our cards.

STEPHANOPOULOS DIVES IN: COMEY ON ABC , APRIL 16, 2018

To secure a revolution with a vote?
Or to let impeachment play itself out?
What would Kennedy, Clinton and Eisenhower
do in these flood lights of sensationalism? At least
one would blitz-bomb a medicine factory
in Africa to divert attention.

Leaking is too delicious to pass by.
For a mystic moment, the leaker rises into
the sky in a nimbus of eagerly-sought inside information
and the world floats below him. He is in-the-know.
He is glorified, and the experience cannot be missed.
He, too, is in The White House. He, too, has shadow power.
He isn't just a guy in a side room who is being
chewed out for one cockamamie reason after another.
And, now, even ordinary citizens, bludgeoned by Trumpomania,
are chastised by Comey for having no moral fiber.

Comey, calm down. You are six foot eight inches tall,
but you're not LeBron James hauling an against-all-odds
victory back to your home town. Or are you?

TRUMP FLIP-FLOPPING NIKKI HALEY, APRIL 17, 2018

Ah, Florida, your Japanese peacefulness,
your aqua seas, my butler, my palm trees...
what a welcome release from Haley's rattled
insubordination and sanction-happy reveries.
I showed her, and what do they call it? "Policy
inconsistencies", as if I don't have enough to do,
tailgating liar Comey and his slimy buddies.
I am going nowhere but up, America,
get over your witchy, stake-burning ways.
I've got more employed golf-caddies
than you have investigative reporters.
I'm not interested in what grandfathers
think of Russia and where Russia's armies
have been. If I am, I warn them about a Syria
strike before anyone pushes a button. I protect
them. This may cause a hash tag situation
but I've got more followers than you can see,
more followers than a deleted bot population.
I've got pizzazz, effrontery. They love me.
Nikki Haley's already fired in my eyes.
She's Hillary's flipside, an uptight woman
acting on her own, a Pence weasel, a speak-
before-you're-spoken-to no one. Thank god,
there's scandal-relieving Mar-a-lago, a place
in the sun with a head of state from Japan
by my side. Thank god, FAANG stocks are up
and no fearless pilot, flying over Syria, died.

DISCONTUATION SYNDROME:
A DEPRESSIVE SPEAKS OUT, APRIL 20, 2018

In a wonky, pill-filled world where nature
recedes behind drawn blinds and inward
melodramas that may, or may not, be true
dominate the Broadway stage of a lonely mind
in a tragicomedy called "Curing Anxiety"
with a single seat in the theater, pulling free
from chemical dependency is unreliable.
Uptown, downtown and cross-town truck
deliveries are too loud. Once-close friends
who don't return texts hang from the ceiling
like a shroud, spun from happier memories.
I'm ice cream to diabetics. I vape, or try to
vape. The point is my moods are inescapable.
I can't disobey my doctor or leave my room.
Forget about art school and Central Park.
My family already knows I don't change
my clothes or go out. Even God is impatient
with me, I suppose, and, without serotonin
intake, the theater will close. I'll lose the stage,
lose my lone seat. Soul-crushing fears within
me will be too severe, too unkind, too unmedical.
I'll miss my only weekly appointment and
skydive into the inevitable.

CHANNELING PUTIN

They think they can downsize Russia,
they think they can crimp our style, they
think, with our history, our sufferance, we'll
roll over like a spotted St. Charles cocker spaniel
in a Gainsborough painting begging for a tea biscuit,
that I don't have a Koch Brothers oligarchy at my
fingertips, that I don't deserve to influence
despots like all superpowers do, that I
can't lure fools into my chamber?

It appears they do. I lean back
against my chair, assessing a chess move,
as if tsars weren't cruel in their emerald yachts
and snows never fell on Leningrad. Can I endure
telling Mother Russia's descendants they're tip-top
patsies? Ambition wearies me. I need to work out.
I want territory, to snatch back what was once
mine. And I have such a paunchy adversary.
Defeating him is not grueling.
It's a pastime.

IV

SKY STUDIES

SKY STUDIES

The sky's horizon, once a line, is now
a fish net falling upon time, its atomizing
blues a brisk blog, yet the sky alone contains
no fog, its violets haven't the infrastructure,

the wifi of bluster and decline. The sky
escapes complaint as a soothing barrier to
foreboding – a non-statistic, an effervescent
ongoing. We glide in its opal vacuums, its

indiscriminate width and height until time
glides out of sight, time with its tantamount
frisson. We like to think the sky listens.
We like being still. Our hours crowd

like a gilded shroud. They stick. The sky
will have none of it, nothing shrill or harrowing.
Each threaded mystery comes unbound under
its arched silence, all commotion seamless.

OVERCAST

The incongruency of anywhere, its minimalizing
chores, becomes a threadbare horizon under the sky's
pinafore. Whisked clouds lace the idyll. Their hasty
shadows mottle the farm fields, the expansive

languor of landscapes. Even water towers are
gridlocked in clusters under such fast-moving shade
as if every month were ankle-deep in April. Clothespin
technicians wrinkle the swans, like overnight

miasmas don't. The daylight hours are red
with accommodation, red and round. Night does
not converse with clouds. They appear to be asleep
rather than abracadabra's of momentary tides inhabiting

rainbows or polishing streets. Their lambent staccato
keeps us alive, or is it awake? Gazing at sunscreen paint?
Clouds, not the sky, embrace change, its mixed-media
of compromise, its hummed secrecy and restraint.

NOCTURNE

You who seldom comply to chain mail
know so well the sky's confusions, the clouds
that set sail under wobbly moons, the musk grays,
the overwrought gales, the planetary lanterns

singular above all seasons that wince and
stiffen. Nightscapes, mauve and maroon, drown
in deep browns, their gusting galleons hazy lean-tos
on windy obsidian. Within this mercurial ado,

its Pessoas of interchangeable forms, the sky
holds viewers captive in luminous elbow room.
Dark pastels reach stationary easels below, painting
the night, its eclipsed shadows. We gather

it knows you, you who are limitless, too,
we guess it wings you through to us in its spell.
Above gallery walls, you're available, a seafarer's
compass no huge wave can ever quell.

UPSWING

A compendium of outtakes lifts
from the camera like linnets in search
of flaxseed. Photo albums shut their sheaves
and return to low, familiar shelves.

A geyser roars in a whisper. The canyon's
etched anthems fall through the floor, yet the
sky, hallucinatory and calming, remains where
it was before. Cities shrink, disappear.

Everyone who ever lived reconvenes
in lofted air. So it seems in the quiet sequel,
in the collapsed blue hologram as paper-thin
as an old print. It seems Siddhartha dwells

in safety above snapshots and Victoria Falls,
the sky a lotus blossom rimming every bodhisattva,
subsuming vows, postures, failings, their maze
of interruptions, into a single illimitable color.

PRECIPITATION

Ruffled gamelans of rain, unconstrained
by all that seems remembered, ting between
splashed pedestrians under obscure clouds.
Today is unshaven, anyone's haven.

Time is like a chaperone tipsy on punch
at an over-stimulating prom. The sky, once
washed-out by neon, is near-flung, like an unread
crib note. The ineffable keeps falling down,

runnelling street curbs with locomotion in
thin streams that invariably stop as more and more
is forgotten. How to bracket this wet weather,
how to dismantle a public fountain, reverse

riverlets of drops as if nothing rueful ever
happened and then stare into the air, the beauty
of revealed creation, day one before Eden, and hear,
as Stephen Hawking, the universal gamelan?

V

AN ELEGY

SKETCHES OF A HARLEQUIN BREAKFASTING WITH GOD

1

My love, broad-backed and musical,
drove a bike and went to school,
then the opera palled
and the faraway Mamba withered
from the world, still Gerswiny, still permissible.
I unfurl my botanical eye
and become a statistic in an audition,
an initial sketch.
My love is breakfasting with a stylish director.
He is an inception in a musical comedy with a pointless ending.
I crush a monkey wrench. I am a lacquered editress
in the ticklish domain.
A certain sadness Zeffirelli overestimated
sounds in the brain
like a cong
thrice dimmed.

2

Seen from Jersey, seen from Jersey,
the world wintertimes on tiered bleachers.
I contradict a shotgun
and the yellow light writes itself.
The instrumental little pain comes back again.
What breakfast are they having in the non-vocal clouds?
Are there daytimes? Are there harpsichords?
Will the plump lily be a god?
Incommunicably tight, the yellow light
greets the insect season overnight.
My love is a sunburn on a cruise, no longer peeling, no longer new,
the years "squid eggs through a microscope"
in the cheap blackness of adieux.

3

My love is drinking orange juice.
He is top rank, musico-dramatic. He is a write-up.
Here, in the shortcomings of design,
I have a juicy salary. I lack distraction.
It is too luscious-looking.
Downcoming concerns wear two neckties,
variants touched by living breath, re-eruptions,
but now it rains, slightly, lightly,
and the daisy-chains come loose, on-and-off friendships.
I see them from a caboose.
The world is near-sensual, a pinch.
Who can complain, Virgil,
who can complain about this?

4

My love sips a cold demitasse.
Does he have men-friends? An abode?
Are the oceanless gulls silk-voiced and repetitive?
It rains, unsimilarly.
Grays grey the featureless trees.
Slate roofs drip in the wet economy.
The world sits and knits.
A cuckoo flies through an estimate, a Pharaoh on television.
My love will bring down the house.
My love will steal the show,
like an evident sea squall, like a one-sided buffalo.
He is breakfasting with Antonioni.
They are discussing "chromatic urbanity,"
or a meditative rodeo
in cat's cradle kliegs–
inconclusive parities, notate, primal,
for the wet world
where everything's been written before,
where virgins are ardent in the ideographs,
ardent and horizontal,
and the Nasdaq soars upward toward Cocteau
with adherence, with afterglow,
into the listening eye,
into vertigo,
the Gallic illuminata.

5

Wetness adores
matters at home or abroad;
the world is surrounded by flying saucers.
Trembling questions reveal a glass hive,
while lesser monologues kiss the strangely bland
on the hand, an overflow,
fauna fauna.
My love clatters the cups;
the porcelain pirouettes, then slumps.
Fleas come out of hiding from within drenched hostas,
the rain has stopped, the *rien* of traffic.
If I knock, you are me. If you knock, I am you.
Across the porcelain hops a geranium.
It will do. On a painted terrain,
leaves waver
as velleities on water in a stream
locked within loops on Ottoman porcelain
designed for a Sultan
or a Sultan's queen.

6

Mod, its kachoos of sexy pants,
was a style. Now it's slipped back a while,
like specialized hairdos above loose teeth.
Dora Maar peeps
through Picasso's paint.
Did she read at home? Did she stay out late?
In back of the spine: another time,
but the eye cannot rotate.
It has been fixed in place by the fist
of The Great Spirit,
though the lynx is less with it
in the gnashed woods.
"Goodbye," Madonna sings, is most powerful.
Goodbye, ocelot. Goodbye, colocollo.

7

The rain, lapidarian,
has come back again, without a word.
The world, bluish and gauzed, gazes through
an interminable pause. It looks
flat, bereft of banditos.
My love takes
a napkin from his lap, which he folds,
and unfolds and refolds.
Is there fire? Is there embroidery?
The un-umbrella'd spiders sleep,
fat in their spider dreams, gnat-happy,
replete of slinking missions.
All is accomplished
here, in the backstep of skeletons,
in the mash of miscellanea.
All is compost below the mirador.
The hostas bloom a single purplish flower
as the crow's cries
paper-airplane the limp sky,
bent as the ragged shoulders of a former gent.
Are mangosteens served on Wednesdays
on a table without legs?
Is the brioche brittle
or consumed?
It is neither evening, nor afternoon.
A stone torso is gored by a lit candle in an art gallery.
That alone is indisputable.

8

Panjandrums nudge me
from my soirees with dripping trees.
We must cut trees down,
according to the authorities who want to cut trees:
we must clear the air of bats,
of bat-winged vanities.
My love will start rehearsals soon.
Crowds will arrive at Hartford,
sculptors from Japan
and Thai Buddhists.
It will be a grand-slam audience,
an ache for the absolute.
Palmy interludes disrupt this oncoming truth.
Crickets copulate below the orange juice.
Tire tracks survive
and are abused by tides of sunrise.
They, too, have a moment,
a paddywhack imprint.
Crows scat,
impatient with swirls of rain.
Time sweeps, like a scarf from a neck, the water's pour.
Spiders unclasp and stretch
in the air's besotted silence
which is now laced
with the reinstated whirr
of parking lots amid conifers,
their outbreeding of bloated earth, of toad's feet
suspended above
damp expectant burrs.

9

Such release, paginal peace,
a blink of sun,
its jaunty palabra for moist mirth
that fans, like Pan, jocular deities with tunes
into the reveries of mosquitoes and men,
and resumes its stolid ephemera,
memos of mania 'ere the tomb:
the scared world's carved scars, its henna-toned tattoos.
Skywise, the pshaws of near-noon
blanch the hostas' latitudes
with determined bees.
Dragonflies await the moist delays
of lawn weddings, their white amoeba-like flux.
Separation, the conundrum of love,
is nipped by vestments in the bud
as ceremonies ingest the nothingness of death,
one by one. The great comeuppance
of belief that keeps all ships
from every reef
under draconian insect wings
above the clipped-green sloping gardens
reseams the fray of longing with the promise of steadfast Penelope
or the stature of olivine in a rain-sloshed tree,
its rattle of cyclic monarchs
and bark-bashed beak-taps.
My love once glimpsed the weary wetted wing
before he glimpsed everything.
They will review him.
They will discuss each shadowed gesture.

10

Ballets seem mechanical these days,
obdurate in the glaze
of new stuff,
yet, a barrage of legs is enough
to stop the clock in a violet symphony.
Blame the Pleiades,
they are nameable and please,
they are Ariadne's diamond trousseau,
they are satin toes.
Long ago, in the gridiron thrusts of early Fall,
parked-car picnics with flasked gin
were prerequisites to costume balls
of Apollonian-padded men...
oh nevermind,
heroes huddle in the thrall,
and recollection
is the whine of time.

11

Denuded now,
I dwell between keys,
a Plexiglas portal no one sees,
an "o" of fogged clarity
or an ovoid with one thin memory.
Something occurred,
like an unplayed score,
but the virile paragons flame no more.
Like lashes of lost rain,
they evaporate
in a thwunk of sun
that comes and comes.
The world hires outriders to police
its race-track hooves.
A virus of televisions curtails the veering words
that once preened, sveltly,
to a rock-bound taper.
My love, also, wrote and drew.
He will have young fans,
Deadhead vans, women who shriek.
He will have the Gap-clad,
hopeful roses.

12

Movie music,
dusk's deliveries–
Clouds bunch as brambles below a faint snow,
the shroud of light a pallid glow,
mute as a mummer in the vaudeville hour.
It has rained and unrained
in the pine-lined bower
where, here and there, puce impatiens' sway,
sheltered by sculpted rows
of streaked-leafed hostas,
where fleas retreat as if to think:
"Shall I tackle a branch or a flower?"
Oceans bob in faraway skeins of loam
in the betwix'd home
of emptied space.
My love shall trace bardic taps
across the stage,
Bojangles in Stratford on Avon
in the opening and reopening nights in Hartford.
Very toney, very too-too.
The sky, its whiskered rain,
is soft and gentle.
The weather, unlike the play, will change.
The director is masterful
and over the hill.
Fleas buzz around his Bowler and cane.

13

The night is satiate–
fallen, felled. A susurrus of bats
ripples its ink wells, the tips of their wings quills,
a velvet calligraphy between leaves.
A slow turning away
from a Beatles-laden yesterday
demurs to Lot's wife.
It is too late to leave, too soon to stay
in the vassitude, in the black lake
stapled to absent swans.
The moon is chopped in half.
Bugs in black-outs snooze amid lax umbra.
The past has swallowed up enough.
Its underglaze does not amaze
the open-eyed.
They request a butterfly, noisy details–
comedy videos that purr.
My love daylessly dreams
of what he's known below the trees,
rocket-kit details,
a white orchid corsage.

Also by Star Black:

Double Time
Watertorn
Balefire
October for Idas
Ghostwood
Stigmata Errata Etcetera by Bill Knott / Artwork by Star Black
Velleity's Shade / Artwork by Bill Knott

The Popular Vote was printed using the fonts Adobe Garamond.

www.saturnaliabooks.org